Adult Colouring Book Series

Volume 5

OWLS

Adult Colouring Book

Creative and Relaxing Art Therapy for Adults

By Edith Brookes

Published in 2016 by
Creative Colours

This Book Belongs To

_____

For Dad. The wise owl of the family Xx.

Introduction

I'm lucky enough to live close to a nature reserve. We see all manner of amazing animals because of this; badgers and foxes are the most common (especially when the trash is out!) But there are some animals that we hear more than we see. For instance, the local woodpecker is quite active in the evening. We also hear the comforting twit-twooing of the owls that live in the forest close by.

Owls are amazing creatures and are often looked upon as being the wisest of all animals. The species is an impressive one, not only for their unique anatomy but also their amazing hunting abilities.

For this particular book, I've included some wonderful owl pictures for you to colour. Each is printed on single-sided paper, making it easier for you to cut them out and frame, without the dreadful decision of having to sacrifice another picture.

So grab those colouring pencils and colour on, but most of all - enjoy!

Edith Brookes

Scribble Page

Test your materials and drawing techniques on this page. Some alcohol felt pens may bleed through the paper so make sure you use a piece of card underneath the picture you're working on, to ensure that there are no leaky-accidents.

Thank you again for purchasing this book. I do hope that you've enjoyed colouring in the pictures provided.

It'd be great if you could write a quick review of this purchase on Amazon. It will only take a couple of minutes of your time and it would be greatly appreciated.

Best wishes & have a great day!

Edith Brookes

Printed in Great Britain
by Amazon